Guess What!

Activity Book 3

with Digital Pack

T0343024

British English

Lynne Marie Robertson

Series Editor: Lesley Koustaff

Shaftesbury Road, Cambridge CB2 8EA, United Kingdom

One Liberty Plaza, 20th Floor, New York, NY 10006, USA

477 Williamstown Road, Port Melbourne, VIC 3207, Australia

314–321, 3rd Floor, Plot 3, Splendor Forum, Jasola District Centre, New Delhi – 110025, India

103 Penang Road, #05–06/07, Visioncrest Commercial, Singapore 238467

Cambridge University Press & Assessment is a department of the University of Cambridge.

We share the University's mission to contribute to society through the pursuit of education, learning and research at the highest international levels of excellence.

www.cambridge.org
Information on this title: www.cambridge.org/9781009798334

First published 2014
Updated edition 2024

20 19 18 17 16 15 14 13 12 11 10 9 8 7 6 5 4 3 2 1

Printed in Dubai by Oriental Press

A catalogue record for this publication is available from the British Library

ISBN 978-1-009-79833-4 Activity Book with Digital Pack Level 3
ISBN 978-1-009-48060-4 Pupil's Book with eBook Level 3
ISBN 978-1-009-79840-2 Teacher's Book with Digital Pack Level 3
ISBN 978-1-107-52807-9 Flashcards Level 3

Additional resources for this publication at www.cambridge.org/guesswhatue

Contents

Welcome

1 **Look and write the names.**

> Anna   Lily   Lucas   Max   Tom

1 _Lucas_
2 _____
3 _____
4 _____
5 _____

2 **Look at activity 1. Read and write *true* or *false*.**

1 Tom likes Art. _true_
2 Anna is ten. _____
3 Max is Lucas's dog. _____
4 Lily's favourite sport is football. _____
5 Lucas's favourite colour is red. _____

My picture dictionary ➡ **Go to page 84: Find and write the new words.**

3 **Read and match.**

1 What's your name?   a I'm nine years old.
2 How old are you?   b My favourite colour is green.
3 What's your favourite colour?   c My name's Bill.
4 Do you like dogs?   d Yes, I can.
5 Have you got a bike?   e Yes, I do.
6 Can you ride a horse?   f No, I haven't.

4 **Answer the questions. Then draw your picture.**

1 What's your name?
   My name is _____

2 How old are you?
_____

3 Have you got a bike?
_____

4 What's your favourite colour?
_____
_____

5 Do you like dogs?
_____

6 Can you play tennis?
_____

Grammar **5**

5 (Think) **Write the months in order. Then answer the question. Use the letters in the boxes to complete the answer.**

1 _J a n u a r y_

2 _F_ [ ] _ _ _ _ _ _

3 _M_ _ _ _ _ _

4 _A_ _ _ _ _ _

5 _M_ _ _

6 _J_ _ _ [ ]

7 _J_ _ [ ] _

8 _A_ _ _ _ _ _

9 _S_ _ _ _ _ _ _ _ _

10 _O_ _ [ ] _ _ _ _

11 _N_ _ [ ] _ _ _ _ _

12 _D_ _ _ _ _ _ _ _

How many months are there?

_ _ W _ _ _ _ _

6 (About Me) **Answer the questions.**

1 What month is it?

_It is_ _____

2 What's your favourite month?

_____

My picture dictionary → Go to page 84: Find and write the new words.

Skills: *Writing*

7 Read the email. Circle the answers to the questions.

Hello!
My name's Jill. I'm(eleven)years old. My birthday is in April.
I've got one brother and one sister. I've got a pet rabbit.
My favourite sport is basketball. What about you?
Jill ☺

1 How old are you?
2 When is your birthday?
3 Have you got any brothers or sisters?
4 Have you got a pet?
5 What's your favourite sport?

8 (About Me) Look at activity 7. Answer the questions.

1 _I'm_ _____
2 _____
3 _____
4 _____
5 _____

9 (About Me) Write an email to a penpal.

Hello!
My name's _____
_____
_____
_____
_____

10 (About Me) Ask and answer with a friend.

How old are you?   I'm eleven years old.

11 Read and number in order.

a. Let's do the treasure hunt together!
Good idea.

b. Treasure Hunt.
Find 7 things in 7 days.
Text 123 to join.
A surprise at the end!

c. It's a mobile phone!
And look at this!

d. Happy Birthday, Lily!
Thanks, Tom. Thanks everyone for your presents.
1

e. What's this present?
I don't know.
Open it, Lily!

f. Dad, can we do this treasure hunt, please?
Yes, of course! It sounds fun.
123 – there!

12 Look at activity 11. Write *yes* or *no*.

1 It's Tom's birthday.   _no_

2 The present is a mobile phone.   _____

3 The treasure hunt is to find 7 things in 5 days.   _____

4 Lily's friends don't want to do the treasure hunt.   _____

5 The treasure hunt sounds fun.   _____

13 **Read and tick the sentences that show the value: work together.**

1 Let's do the treasure hunt together. ✓   4 Good idea. ☐

2 Let's find my dog. ☐   5 Let's tidy up. ☐

3 I like card games. ☐   6 I'm playing basketball. ☐

14 **Circle the words that sound like *snake*.**

c<u>a</u>t	tr<u>ai</u>n	w<u>a</u>ter	f<u>a</u>rm
(sn<u>a</u>ke)	dr<u>a</u>w	g<u>a</u>me	pl<u>a</u>nt
p<u>a</u>rk	r<u>a</u>bbit	p<u>ai</u>nt	c<u>a</u>mera
b<u>a</u>rn	m<u>a</u>n	c<u>a</u>ke	t<u>ai</u>l
f<u>a</u>n	g<u>a</u>rden	b<u>a</u>th	b<u>a</u>ll

What can you see in a landscape painting?

1 **Look and match.**

(birds)　　(boat)　　(forest)　　(mountain)

(plants)　　(river)　　(sea)　　(waterfall)

2 **Draw two landscapes.**

Draw a river.
Draw some trees behind it.
Draw a boat and three ducks on the river.

Draw four tall trees in a forest.
Draw some plants between the trees.
Draw an animal in the forest.

Evaluation

1 Do the word puzzle.

Down ↓

①  ②

④

```
        1
        T
        O   4
    2   3 M ___ ___
    ___     ___
5   ___ ___ ___ ___
    ___
```

Across →

③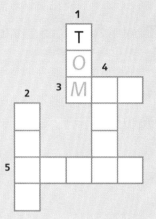

⑤

2 About Me **Find and write the questions. Then answer.**

1 are / old / you? / How

<u>How old are you?</u>

<u>I'm</u>

2 your / When's / birthday?

_____

_____

3 swim? / you / Can

_____

_____

4 colour? / your / What's / favourite

_____

_____

_____

5 you / Have / a / got / brother?

_____

_____

3 About Me **Complete the sentences about this unit.**

1 I can talk about _____ .

2 I can write about _____ .

3 My favourite part is _____ .

4 **Guess who it is.**

Go to page 93 and circle the answer.

1 In the garden

1 Look and guess. Then find and write the words.

l l r i a r p a e c t
caterpillar

t u b y t f l e r
_____

s a g r s
_____

s e r t o o t i
_____

a i s l n
_____

e a g i n u g i p
_____

r e f w o l
_____

e r e t
_____

t r i b a b
_____

f e l a
_____

2 Write the words from activity 1 on the lists.

Animals	Plants
caterpillar	*grass*

My picture dictionary → Go to page 85: Find and write the new words.

3 **Look and circle the words.**

4 **Look and complete the sentences. Then colour the animals.**

Her Her His Our | big big small small

Her pet is _small_ and yellow.

_____ pet is _____ and grey.

_____ pet is _____ and brown.

_____ pet is _____ and orange.

5 Look and circle the questions and answers.

1 (What's that?)
What are those?

a (It's a snail.)
They're snails.

2 What's that?
What are those?

b It's a flower.
They're flowers.

3 What's that?
What are those?

c It's a tortoise.
They're tortoises.

4 What's that?
What are those?

d It's a bird.
They're birds.

5 What's that?
What are those?

e It's a leaf.
They're leaves.

6 Look and write the questions and answers.

~~butterflies~~   caterpillar   spider   trees

1 _What are those?_

They're butterflies.

2 _What's that?_

3 _____

_____

4 _____

_____

Skills: *Writing*

7 **Read the paragraph and write the words.**

> butterflies   leaves   ~~small~~   tree   white

My favourite bug is a caterpillar. Caterpillars are ¹____small____ . I like black
and ²_____ caterpillars. You can see a caterpillar on a ³_____ .
The caterpillar eats the green ⁴_____ . Beautiful ⁵_____ come
from caterpillars.

8 (About Me) **Answer the questions.**

1   What's your favourite bug?
    My favourite bug is _____

2   What colour is it?
    _____

3   Is it big or small or beautiful?
    _____

4   Where can you see it?
    _____

9 (About Me) **Write about your favourite bug.**

My favourite bug _____

_____

_____

_____

_____

_____

10 (About Me) **Ask and answer with a friend.**

> What's your favourite animal?   My favourite animal is a horse.

11 Read and match.

1	Not now, Anna.	**3**	Are those ears and a tail?
2	Sorry, Anna. Thank you.	**4**	Can we borrow it, please?

12 Look at activity 11. Answer the questions.

1 What do they see behind the tree?   *Ears and a tail.*

2 What animal is behind the tree?   _____

3 What animal has Anna got?   _____

4 What can they do with it?   _____

5 Who is sorry?   _____

13 Look and write the questions and answers. Then tick the picture that shows the value: respect and listen to others.

Can I help?   Yes, you can. Thank you.   Can I help?   Not now.

14 Write the words with the same sound in the lists.

cake   tree   paint   leaf   make   jeans
sleep   eat   tail   chimpanzee   train   snake

cake

tree

What types of habitats are there?

1 **Write the names of the habitats. Then circle the two correct sentences.**

> desert   grassland   ~~rainforest~~   tundra

1 rainforest

It's a hot place.
There are lots of trees and leaves.
Lions live here.

It's a hot place.
Monkeys live here.
There is a lot of grass.

It's a cold place.
There are lots of trees.
Bears live here.

There is little water.
Snakes and spiders live here.
There are lots of fish.

2 **Draw and write about a habitat in your country.**

It's a _____ place. There are lots of _____. _____ live here.

Evaluation

1 Find and write the words.

1 *What's that?*
It's a flower.

2 _____
They're leaves.

3 _____
They're caterpillars.

4 _____
It's a butterfly.

5 _____
It's grass.

2 Look and write the words.

| ~~My~~ Your Our Their | ~~tortoise~~ fish rabbit snail | ~~small~~ big grey green |

____*My*____ *tortoise*   _____   _____   _____
is ___*small*___ .   is _____ .   is _____ .   is _____ .

3 About Me Complete the sentences about this unit.

1 I can talk about _____ .

2 I can write about _____ .

3 My favourite part is _____ .

4 Puzzle Guess what it is.

Go to page 93 and circle the answer.

2 At school

1 Look and number the picture.

1 playground
2 gym
3 Science room
4 sports field
5 dining hall
6 Art room
7 library
8 Music room
9 reception
10 classroom

2 (Think) Look at activity 1. Read the sentences and write the words.

1 You can paint pictures in this room. _____Art room_____

2 There are desks and chairs in this room. _____

3 You can eat lunch in this room. _____

4 You have a Science lesson in this room. _____

5 You can run, jump and dance in this room. _____

6 You go here when you visit the school. _____

7 You can play football here. _____

8 You can play outside here. _____

9 You can read books here. _____

10 You can sing here. _____

My picture dictionary → Go to page 86: Find and write the new words.

3 Look and circle the answers.

We're / They're on the sports field.

We're / They're in the Art room.

We're / They're in the Science room.

We're / They're in the classroom.

4 Look and complete the questions and answers.

We're in the library!

Hello!

Hi!

1 Where are ___they___ ? _____ in the reception.

2 Where are _____ ? ___We're___ in the library.

3 Where are _____ ? _____ in the gym.

4 Where are _____ ? _____ in the Music room.

5 Where are _____ ? _____ in the playground.

5 Read and match.

a They're playing basketball.

b They're playing football.

c We're playing basketball.

d We're playing football.

6 Look and write the questions and answers.

1 _What are you doing?_   _We're_ _____

2 _____   _They're_ _____

3 _____   _____

4 _____   _____

Skills: *Writing*

7 Read the text. Circle the answers to the questions.

My school is (small.) There are six classrooms, a library and a big playground.

I like the library, but my favourite room is the gym. There are **18** children

in my class. My favourite lesson is English.

1 Is your school big or small?
2 What rooms and places are in your school?
3 What is your favourite room?
4 How many children are in your class?
5 What is your favourite lesson?

8 (About Me) Look at activity 7. Answer the questions.

1 *My school is* _____

2 _____

3 _____

4 _____

5 _____

9 (About Me) Write a description of your school.

My school _____

_____

_____

_____

_____

_____

_____

10 (About Me) Ask and answer with a friend.

What's your favourite lesson?   My favourite lesson is Science.

11 Read and write the words.

Thank you!　　pick up　　~~litter~~　　Listen!

What are they doing?

They're picking up _litter_ . Let's help.

Hi, Aunt Pat. Can we help?

Yes, please. Can you _____ this litter?

Come on, Lily!

Wait! _____ What's that?

Thanks for your help! You can have the radio.

_____

12 Look at activity 11. Write *yes* or *no*.

1	Dad and Aunt Pat are in the gym.	_no_
2	Aunt Pat is picking up litter.	
3	The children don't help.	
4	Lily is listening to the radio.	
5	Aunt Pat wants the radio.	

13 Look and tick the pictures that show the value: keep your environment clean.

14 Circle the words that sound like *tiger*.

What materials can we recycle?

1 **Look and match.**

2 **Design two recycling bins for your school.**

Where is it? _____

_____

What can children put in it? _____

_____

Where is it? _____

_____

What can children put in it? _____

_____

Evaluation

1 **Look and answer the questions.**

1 Where are we? _We're in the reception._

2 What are we doing? _____

3 Where are the boys? _____

4 What are they doing? _____

5 Where are the girls? _____

6 What are they doing? _____

7 Where are the teachers? _____

8 What are they doing? _____

2 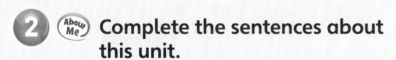 **Complete the sentences about this unit.**

1 I can talk about _____ .

2 I can write about _____ .

3 My favourite part is _____ .

3  **Guess what it is.**

Go to page 93 and circle the answer.

Review Units 1 and 2

1 Look and find the numbers. Answer the questions.

1 Where are they? *They're in the Science room.*

2 What are those? _____

3 What is he doing? _____

4 What are those? _____

5 What are they doing? _____

6 Where are they? _____

7 What's that? _____

8 What's that? _____

2 Think Find 11 months ↓ →. Then answer the question.

N	O	V	E	M	B	E	R	T	J	S	F	G	M
A	C	B	Z	A	P	Y	E	J	U	N	E	K	A
W	T	A	Q	Y	N	A	C	I	L	T	B	O	R
B	O	N	J	A	N	U	A	R	Y	S	R	I	C
K	B	U	P	B	T	A	N	G	K	W	U	L	H
D	E	C	E	M	B	E	R	X	A	C	A	G	M
O	R	O	C	G	M	A	I	O	A	P	R	I	L
P	B	Y	A	U	G	U	S	T	W	B	Y	J	D

One month is not in the puzzle. What month is it?

_____

3 **Look and write the questions.**

1 _What's her name?_   It's Kate.

2 _____ It's in May.

3 _____ Her favourite colour is pink.

4 _Who are they?_   They're my cousins.

5 _____ They're in the park.

6 _____ They're flying a kite.

4 **Look at the photos in activity 3. Complete the sentences.**

1   _His T-shirt_   is yellow.   3 _____ are blue.

2 _____ is pink.   4 _____ is a plane.

5 **Think** **Answer the questions.**

> a bird   a butterfly   a caterpillar   a dining hall
> February   grass   ~~a guinea pig~~   a library

1 These eat leaves. What are they?   _A guinea pig_   and _____

2 You can eat here. Where is it? _____

3 You can read books here. Where is it? _____

4 These can fly. What are they? _____ and _____

5 This has 8 letters. What month is it? _____

6 This is a plant. What is it? _____

3 School days

1 Write the days of the week.

	n a d y M o	a u s d e T y	s d a y d e n W e
	Monday		
Sue			
Dan			

Dan   Sue

	y h r d u T s a	i a y F d r	y r t d S a a u	y S n d u a
Sue				
Dan				

2 Look at activity 1. Write *yes* or *no*.

1 She's got Maths on Thursday. _____ yes

2 He's got Gym on Friday. _____

3 She's got Art on Monday. _____

4 He's got football club on Saturday. _____

5 She's got computer club on Sunday. _____

3 Look at activity 1. Write the sentences.

1 Monday: *She's got Music and he's got Science.* _____

2 Tuesday: _____

3 Wednesday: _____

4 Thursday: _____

5 Friday: _____

My picture dictionary **Go to page 87: Find and write the new words.**

4 **Look and follow. Then complete the questions and answers.**

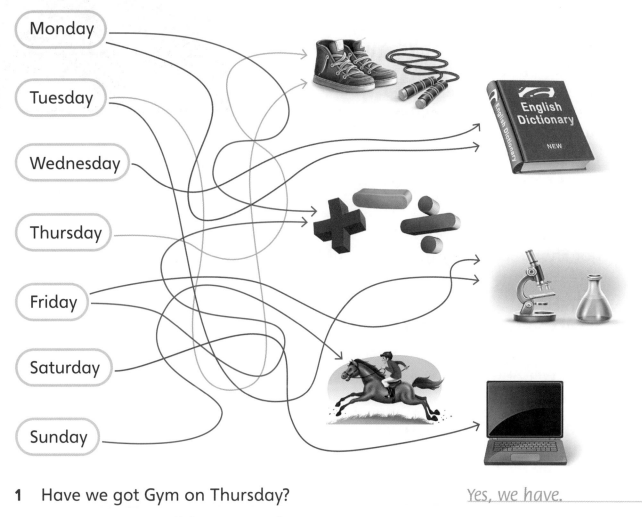

1 Have we got Gym on Thursday?   _Yes, we have._

2 Have we got English on Saturday?   _____

3 Have we got Maths on Monday?   _____

4 _____ Science on Friday?   _____

5 _____ computer club on Sunday?   _____

6 _____ horse riding club on Sunday?   _____

5 **Look at activity 4. Complete the sentences.**

1 _We haven't got_ Maths on Thursday.

2 _____ English on Monday and Wednesday.

3 _____ Science on Tuesday and Friday.

4 _____ horse riding club on Thursday.

5 _____ computer club on Saturday.

6 _____ Gym on Monday and Friday.

6 **Think Read and complete Josh's day.**

Monica
What lessons have you got on Tuesday?

Josh
We've got Gym, Science and Art in the morning. Gym is before Science. Art is after Science.

Monica
What lessons have you got in the afternoon?

Josh
We've got English and Maths. We've got English after lunch. We've got Maths after English.

Monica
Have you got a club after school?

Josh
Yes, I've got football club in the evening.

Josh   Monica

Tuesday

morning

1 _____

2 _____ *Science*

3 _____

LUNCH

afternoon

4 _____

5 _____

evening

6 _____

7 **Look at activity 6. Write the answers.**

1 What lesson has Josh got after Gym?

   He's got Science after Gym.

2 What lesson has Josh got after lunch?

   _____

3 What lesson has Josh got before lunch?

   _____

4 What lesson has Josh got before Maths?

   _____

8 **About Me Choose a day from your timetable. Answer the questions.**

1 What lessons have you got in the morning?

   I've got _____

2 What lessons have you got in the afternoon?

   _____

3 Have you got a club after school?

   _____

Skills: *Writing*

9 **Read the paragraph and write the words.**

horse   club   morning   ~~Saturday~~   Music   competitions

My favourite day of the week is ¹ _____Saturday_____ . I've got a ² _____
lesson in the ³ _____ . I've got photo ⁴ _____ in the
afternoon. In the evening I've got a ⁵ _____ riding lesson and
a dance competition. I like ⁶ _____ .

10 (About Me) **Answer the questions.**

1   What's your favourite day of the week?
    My favourite day is _____

2   What have you got in the morning?

    _____

3   What have you got in the afternoon?

    _____

4   What have you got in the evening?

    _____

11 (About Me) **Write about your favourite day.**

My favourite _____

_____

_____

_____

_____

12 (About Me) **Ask and answer with a friend.**

Have you got any clubs this week?

Yes, I've got computer club on Thursday.

13 Read and number in order.

a — It's very good, Tom. / What do you think, Max?

b — We can't take a photo of the painting. / What can we do now? / I've got an idea!

c — Is the art gallery open on Saturdays? / Yes, it is. / Come on. Let's go!

d — Are you OK, Tom? / Yes, I'm fine. Don't worry.

e — OK. Here we are. / Now where's the painting? / Over there!

f — What day is it today? / It's Saturday. / Find this painting. / Great! I like Art. Let's go to the art gallery. / 1

14 Look at activity 13. Answer the questions.

1 Who likes Art? _Tom._____

2 What is open on Saturdays? _____

3 What can't they do? _____

4 What animal is in the painting? _____

5 What does Tom do? _____

15 **Look and tick the pictures that show the value: be resourceful.**

16 **Colour the words that sound like *goat*. Then answer the question.**

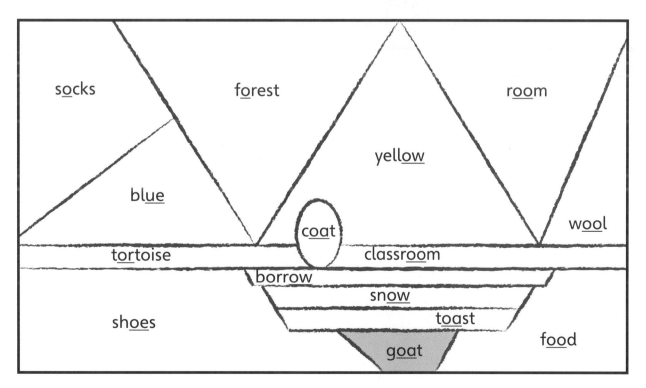

socks   forest   room

yellow

blue

coat   wool

tortoise   classroom

borrow

snow

shoes   toast

food

goat

What's in the picture? _____

Which animals are nocturnal?

1 Read and tick the sentences that are true for nocturnal animals.

1 It finds food and eats at night. ☑

2 It likes running and flying in the day. ☐

3 It likes playing in the evening and at night. ☐

4 It sleeps in the morning and afternoon. ☐

2 Draw and label one animal in each box in the table.
Then write sentences about each animal.

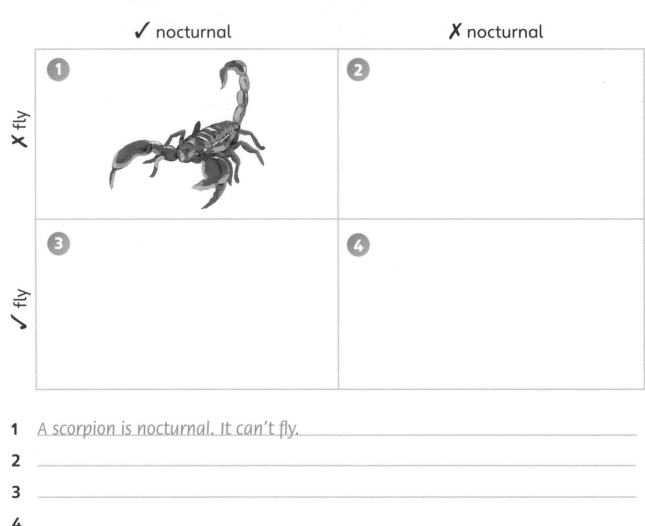

✓ nocturnal   ✗ nocturnal

	✓ nocturnal	✗ nocturnal
✗ fly	1	2
✓ fly	3	4

1 _A scorpion is nocturnal. It can't fly._

2

3

4

Evaluation

Emily   Jacob

1 **Write the days of the week in the diary and answer the questions.**

Thursday	**Sa**
10:00 Art	3:00 Gym competition
2:00 English test	
6:00 football club	
F	**S**
9:00 Gym	10:00 photo club
1:00 Science	12:00 lunch with Grandma

1 Have you got Art on Friday?   _No, we haven't._

2 Have you got Art on Thursday?   _____

3 Have you got a Maths test on Thursday?   _____

4 Have you got a Gym competition on Saturday?   _____

2 **Look at activity 1. Answer the questions about Emily.**

1 Look at Thursday. What has she got in the morning?   _She's got Art._

2 Look at Thursday. What has she got in the evening?   _____

3 Look at Friday. What has she got in the morning?   _____

4 Look at Friday. What has she got in the afternoon?   _____

5 Look at Sunday. What has she got before lunch?   _____

3 **Complete the sentences about this unit.**

1 I can talk about _____ .

2 I can write about _____ .

3 My favourite part is _____ .

4 **Guess what it is.**

Go to page 93 and circle the answer.

4 My day

1 Look and write the answers.

> clean your teeth   get up   go to bed   ~~go to school~~
> have breakfast   have dinner   have lunch   have a shower

1 _go to school_

2 _____

3 _____

4 _____

5 _____

6 _____

7 _____

8 _____

2 (About Me) Look at activity 1. Write six sentences about your day.

1 I _____get dressed_____ in the morning.

2 I _____

3 _____ in the afternoon.

4 _____ in the evening.

5 _____

6 _____

My picture dictionary → Go to page 88: Find and write the new words.

3 Read and match.

1 I get dressed at seven o'clock.

2 I go to school at eight o'clock.

3 I eat lunch at twelve o'clock.

4 I go home at half past three.

5 I eat dinner at half past seven.

6 I go to bed at half past nine.

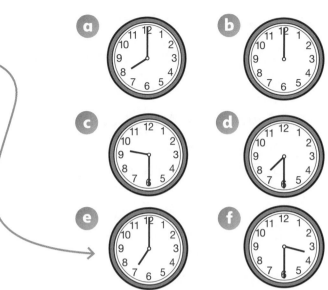

4 Look and complete the sentences.

1 I _____get up_____ at _____half past seven_____ .

2 I _____ at _____ .

3 I _____ at _____ .

4 I _____ at _____ .

5 I _____ at _____ .

6 I _____ at _____ .

5 (About Me) Write sentences and draw the times.

1 I _have breakfast_ at _____ .

2 I _____ at _____ .

3 I _____ at _____ .

4 I _____ at _____ .

6 (Think) **Read and answer the questions.**

Ken: What time do you get up?
Eva: I get up at half past seven.
Ken: So do I.
Maya: I don't. I get up at seven o'clock.

Maya: What time do you go to bed?
Ken: I go to bed at nine o'clock.
Eva: I don't. I go to bed at half past eight.
Maya: So do I.

Maya   Eva   Ken

1 Who gets up at seven o'clock?   _____Maya_____
2 Who gets up at half past seven?   _____ and _____
3 Who goes to bed at half past eight?   _____ and _____
4 Who goes to bed at nine o'clock?   _____

7 **Look and complete the sentences.**

1   What time do you have dinner?

I __have dinner__ at __seven o'clock__ .

So do I.   I don't.

2   What time do you have breakfast?

I _____ at _____ .

I _____ at _____ .

8 (About Me) **Ask and answer with two friends.**

I get up at …   So do I.   I don't. I get up at …

Skills: *Writing*

9 (About Me) **Write a questionnaire about a healthy lifestyle. Then ask a friend.**

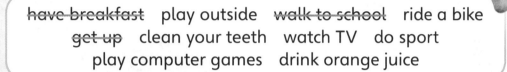

~~have breakfast~~   play outside   ~~walk to school~~   ride a bike
~~get up~~   clean your teeth   watch TV   do sport
play computer games   drink orange juice

Yes / No

1   Do you have breakfast every day? _____   _____

2   Do you walk to school in the morning? _____   _____

3   Do you like getting up early? _____   _____

4   _____   _____

5   _____   _____

6   _____   _____

7   _____   _____

8   _____   _____

9   _____   _____

10   _____   _____

10 (About Me) **Ask and answer with a friend.**

Do you have a healthy lifestyle?   Yes, I do. I walk to school every day.

11 Read and match.

1 I can do the race!
2 The first prize is a watch!
3 Thanks! Swimming is fun!
4 And the winner is ... Lucas!

12 Look at activity 11. Circle the answers.

1 Lucas does _____ .
   a a swimming club   **b** a swimming race   **c** the first prize

2 Lucas thinks swimming is _____ .
   a fun   **b** great   **c** nice

3 Lucas wins _____ .
   a a present   **b** a test   **c** a prize

4 The prize is _____ .
   a a watch   **b** a race   **c** swimming lessons

13 Tick the activities that show the value: take exercise.

1 do a bike race	✓	5 go to bed early	☐
2 go to baseball club	☐	6 go roller skating	☐
3 have a Maths test	☐	7 have a shower	☐
4 play in a tennis competition	☐	8 do sport after school	☐

14 Circle the words that sound like *blue*.

START!

blue	equals	snow	jump	toast	sausage
turn	June	run	goat	excuse	plus
yellow	mouth	shoots	chew	duck	room

FINISH!

What's the time around the world?

1 **Look and answer the questions.**

1 What time is it in Buenos Aires?

It's ___*eight o'clock*___ in the morning

2 What time is it in London?

It's _____ in the afternoon.

3 What time is it in Dubai?

It's _____ .

4 What time is it in Shanghai?

It's _____ .

2 **Draw a picture and write sentences.**

1 I _____ at eight o'clock in the morning.

2 I _____
_____ .

3 I _____
_____ .

4 I _____
_____ .

Evaluation

1 **Look and complete the questions and answers.**

1 What time do you get up?

I get up at half past six.

2 What time do you get dressed?

_____

3 _____

I go to school at eight o'clock.

4 _____

I have dinner at half past seven.

5 What time do you clean your teeth?

_____

6 _____

I go to bed at nine o'clock.

2 (About Me) **Look at activity 1. Write sentences. Start with _So do I_ or _I don't_.**

1 So do I. I get up at half past six.

2 _____

3 _____

4 _____

5 _____

6 _____

3 (About Me) **Complete the sentences about this unit.**

1 I can talk about _____ .

2 I can write about _____ .

3 My favourite part is _____ .

4 (Puzzle) **Guess what it is.**

Go to page 93 and circle the answer.

Review Units 3 and 4

1 Look and complete the sentences about my day.

after lunch   after school   at four o'clock
~~at nine o'clock~~   at half past six   at ten o'clock

1   I go to school _at nine o'clock_ .
2   We've got Maths _____ .
3   We've got Art _____ .
4   We've got tennis club _____ .
5   I go home _____ .
6   I have dinner _____ .

2 (About Me) Write questions and answers.

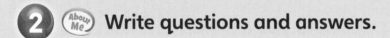
~~get up~~   go to bed   have breakfast | ~~on Monday~~   on Saturday   on Sunday

1   _What time do you get up on Monday?_
    I get up _____
2   _____
    _____
3   _____
    _____
4   _____
    _____

3 **Find the words ↓ →. Use the words to complete the verbs.**

get _dressed_

clean your _____

B	H	F	D	T	E	E	T	H
R	W	V	I	P	K	E	X	M
E	L	U	N	C	H	L	U	S
A	O	Y	N	C	G	B	A	C
K	D	R	E	S	S	E	D	H
F	M	E	R	B	O	D	C	O
A	Z	R	W	E	G	H	H	O
S	H	O	W	E	R	Q	R	L
T	X	L	B	A	U	P	C	Z

have a _____

have _____

go to _____

have _____

have _____

go to _____

4 **Answer the questions.**

1   What day starts with the letter M?   _Monday_

2   What day has nine letters?   _____

3   What day comes after Thursday?   _____

4   What day comes before Sunday?   _____

5   What day has the letter H in it?   _____

6   What day sounds like Monday?   _____

7   Put these letters in order: yadsuTe.   _____

5 Home time

1 Look and match.

a   listen to music

b   eat a sandwich

c   do the dishes

d   read a book

e   drink juice

f   make a cake

g   watch TV

h   wash the car

2 Look at activity 1. Complete the sentences.

1   Look at picture 1.   He's _reading a book_ .

2   Look at picture 2.   He's _____ .

3   Look at picture 4.   She's _____ .

4   Look at picture 6.   She's _____ .

5   Look at picture 7.   He's _____ .

3 Answer the questions.

1   Do you like listening to music? _____

2   Do you like playing on the computer? _____

3   Do you like doing homework? _____

My picture dictionary → Go to page 89: Find and write the new words.

4 Read and match.

1 I love making cakes.

2 My mum likes listening to music.

3 My sister enjoys doing homework.

4 My brother doesn't enjoy playing this game on the computer.

5 My dad doesn't like doing the dishes.

5 Look and complete the sentences.

like   love   doesn't enjoy   ~~doesn't like~~ | ~~drink~~   read   wash   watch

1 He _doesn't like drinking_ juice.

2 She _____ books.

3 He _____ TV.

4 She _____ the car.

6 Write about your friend.

Name: _____

1 _____ loves _____ .

2 _____ likes _____ .

3 _____ doesn't enjoy _____ .

Grammar **49**

7 Look and complete the questions. Then circle the answers.

1 Does he like _____reading books_____ ? (Yes, he does.) / No, he doesn't.

2 Does she enjoy _____ ? Yes, she does. / No, she doesn't.

3 Does she like _____ ? Yes, she does. / No, she doesn't.

4 Does he like _____ ? Yes, he does. / No, he doesn't.

5 Does he enjoy _____ ? Yes, he does. / No, he doesn't.

6 Does she like _____ ? Yes, she does. / No, she doesn't.

8 (Think) Look and complete the questions and answers. Then draw.

Does she enjoy ___making___ a cake?

No, __she doesn't__ .

_____ enjoy _____ TV?

No, _____ .

_____ love _____
on the computer?

Yes, _____ .

_____ like _____
homework?

Yes, _____ .

Skills: *Writing*

9 Read the paragraph and write the words.

> love eating   enjoy tidying   don't like doing   enjoy washing   ~~like making~~

I am helpful at home. In the morning, I ¹___like making___ cakes and
I ²_____ them! I ³_____ my bedroom too.
In the afternoon, I am helpful. I ⁴_____ the dog or the car.
After dinner, I am not helpful. I ⁵_____ the dishes!

10 (About Me) Answer the questions.

1 What do you enjoy tidying?
   _I enjoy_____

2 What do you like washing?
   _____

3 What do you like making?
   _____

4 What do you love doing?
   _____

5 What don't you like doing?
   _____

11 (About Me) Write about being helpful at home.

_I am helpful at home. I like_____
_____
_____
_____

12 (About Me) Ask and answer with a friend.

> Do you like tidying your bedroom?   Yes, I do.

13 Read and write the words.

> need   Watch out   so sorry   ~~likes making~~

a My Aunt Pat _likes making_ cakes.

Find a chocolate cake.

Great! Let's go to her house!

b What do we _____ ?

Eggs, milk, chocolate …

c _____ , Lucas!

Oh no!

d Oh dear! I'm _____ .

Me too!

14 Look at activity 13. Answer the questions.

1 Where are the children going?   _Aunt Pat's house._

2 Does Aunt Pat like making cakes?   _____

3 What do they need to make the cake?   _____

4 What does Lucas drop?   _____

5 Who's sorry?   _____

15 Look and tick the picture that shows the value: show forgiveness.

16 Colour the words that sound like *teeth*. Then answer the question.

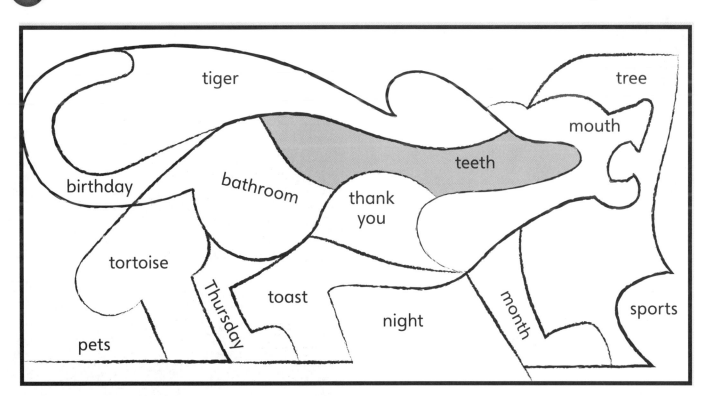

What's this animal? _____

Where do people live?

1 **Find the words and write under the pictures.**

~~wont~~ llivgea ytic ouidecyrtns

town

2 **Look and complete the sentences.**

café houses riding shops supermarket town ~~village~~ walking

In the ¹ _village_ there
is a small ² _____ . There
are two ³ _____ . People
like ⁴ _____ their bikes there.

In the ⁵ _____ there are
a lot of ⁶ _____ and some
shops. You can buy food at the
⁷ _____ . A lot of people
are ⁸ _____ in the street.

Evaluation

1 **Read and match. Then answer the questions.**

Tom

Cara

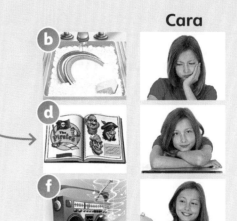

1 read a book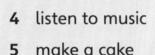
2 do the dishes
3 do homework
4 listen to music
5 make a cake
6 drink juice

1 Does she like reading a book? _Yes, she does._
2 Does she love doing the dishes? _____
3 Does he like doing homework? _____
4 Does he enjoy drinking juice? _____

2 **Look at activity 1. Complete the sentences.**

1 Tom enjoys _doing homework_ .
2 Tom loves _____ , but he doesn't like _____ .
3 Cara loves _____ .
4 Cara doesn't enjoy _____ , but she likes _____ .

3 **Complete the sentences about this unit.**

1 I can talk about _____ .
2 I can write about _____ .
3 My favourite part is _____ .

4 **Guess what it is.**

Go to page 93 and circle the answer.

6 Hobbies

1 Look and number the picture.

1. play volleyball
2. make films
3. do gymnastics
4. play the guitar
5. play table tennis
6. play the recorder

2 Look and write the words.

make   do   ~~play~~   play | models   ~~badminton~~   the piano   karate

1. play badminton
2.
3.
4.

3 Think Write the words from activities 1 and 2 on the lists.

Crafts	Music	Sports
make films		

 My picture dictionary ➡ Go to page 90: Find and write the new words.

4 **Look and follow. Then write *true* or *false*.**

Dan   Anna   Claire   Jamie   May

before school   morning   after lunch   afternoon   evening

1   Dan plays the recorder before school.   *false*

2   Anna does gymnastics in the afternoon.   _____

3   Claire plays volleyball in the evening.   _____

4   Jamie makes models in the morning.   _____

5   May plays the guitar before school.   _____

5 **Look at activity 4. Complete the sentences.**

1   Dan *doesn't play the recorder* before school.

2   Anna _____ in the afternoon.

3   Claire _____ in the evening.

4   Jamie _____ in the morning.

5   May _____ before school.

6 **Look and read. Then answer the questions.**

Hi, Jack. Baseball game on Saturday morning.

Jack, remember model club is Tuesday afternoon. Ben

Hello, Jack. Don't forget gymnastics club Thursday morning before school. Mum

Ella, see you Thursday evening for your piano lesson.

Hi, Ella. Don't forget film club is Friday evening! Amy

Ella. Remember karate club Sunday morning. Dad

1   Does Jack play baseball on Saturdays?   _Yes, he does._
2   Does Ella play the piano in the afternoon?   _____
3   Does Jack make models in the evening?   _____
4   Does Ella make films on Sundays?   _____
5   Does Jack do gymnastics before school?   _____
6   Does Ella do karate on Sundays?   _____

7 **Write questions about Jack and Ella.**

do gymnastics   make films   make models
~~play the guitar~~   play the piano   play volleyball

1   ___Does___ Jack _play the guitar_ on Saturdays? No, he doesn't.
2   _____ Ella _____ on Thursdays? Yes, she does.
3   _____ Jack _____ on Thursdays? Yes, he does.
4   _____ Ella _____ in the evening? Yes, she does.
5   _____ Jack _____ in the afternoon? Yes, he does.
6   _____ Ella _____ on Sundays? No, she doesn't.

Skills: *Writing*

8 **Read the paragraph and write the words.**

after school   competitions   drink   hungry   ~~swimming~~   afternoon

My favourite sport is ¹___swimming___ . I swim every Saturday and Sunday
²_____ . Sometimes there are ³_____ . I am always
⁴_____ after swimming! I eat a sandwich and ⁵_____
a glass of milk. I enjoy playing tennis too. We play ⁶_____
on Friday.

9 **(About Me) Answer the questions.**

1 What is your favourite sport?

My favourite sport is _____

2 When do you do it?

_____

3 Are there any competitions?

_____

4 What do you eat and drink after playing sport?

_____

10 **(About Me) Write about your favourite sport.**

My favourite sport _____

_____

_____

_____

_____

_____

11 **(About Me) Ask and answer with a friend.**

What's your favourite sport?   My favourite sport is horse riding.

12 Read and number in order.

a

Well done, Lucas!

This is fun!

b

Hi, Lily. Come and play the guitar with me!

OK, great!

c

Where can we get a guitar?

Let's ask my cousin, Kim. She plays in a band.

1

d

Here, Lucas. Do you want to play the guitar too?

No, I'm sorry. I can't play!

Come on, Lucas! Try it.

e

Practise every day, Lucas.

f

Oh dear!

You can do it, Lucas!

13 Look at activity 12. Circle the answers.

1   Who plays in a band?
    a Tom's cousin   b Lily's cousin   c Lily

2   Who wants to play guitar with Kim?
    a Lily   b Anna   c Tom

3   What can't Lucas do?
    a play in a band   b find a guitar   c play the guitar

4   What is fun for Lucas?
    a watching Kim   b trying new things   c playing in a band

5   What does Kim want Lucas to do every day?
    a practise the guitar   b play in Kim's band   c try new things

14 **Look and tick the pictures that show the value: try new things.**

15 **Circle the words that sound like *shark*.**

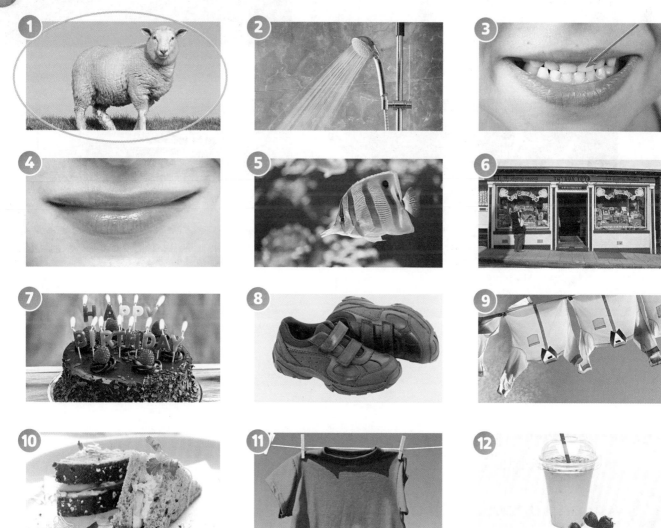

What type of musical instrument is it?

1 **Find the words and write under the pictures.**

girstn srabs sserciupon ~~wwddinoo~~

woodwind

2 **Complete the sentences.**

1 The drum _____ is a percussion instrument _____ .

2 The guitar _____ .

3 The piano _____ .

4 The recorder _____ .

3 **Ask and answer with a friend.**

What instrument do you like?   I like the piano!

Evaluation

1 **Look and complete the Venn diagram. Then answer the questions.**

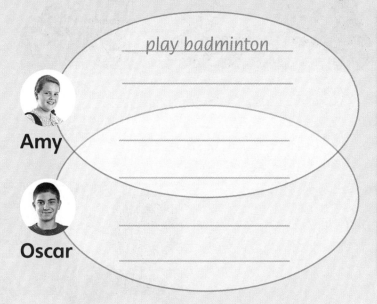

play badminton

_____

Amy

_____

_____

Oscar

_____

Day	Amy	Oscar
Monday morning		
Tuesday after school		
Thursday afternoon		
Friday evening		

1 Does Amy play the piano on Tuesdays? *Yes, she does.*

2 Does Oscar play the piano on Tuesdays? _____

3 Does Amy do karate on Fridays? _____

4 Does Oscar do karate on Tuesdays? _____

2 **Look at activity 1. Complete the sentences about Oscar.**

1 *He doesn't play* table tennis after school.

2 _____ karate in the morning.

3 _____ gymnastics on Wednesdays.

4 _____ the piano on Fridays.

3 (About Me) **Complete the sentences about this unit.**

1 I can talk about _____ .

2 I can write about _____ .

3 My favourite part is _____ .

4 (Puzzle) **Guess what it is.**

Go to page 93 and circle the answer.

Review Units 5 and 6

1 Look and answer the questions.

Jade	☹	☺	☺	☺
Ben	☺	☹	☹	☺

1 Does Ben enjoy playing table tennis? _Yes, he does._

2 Does Jade like playing table tennis? _____

3 Does Ben like reading? _____

4 Does Jade love listening to music? _____

5 Does Ben enjoy playing the guitar? _____

6 Does Jade love playing the guitar? _____

Ben   Jade

2 Look at activity 1. Complete the sentences.

1 Jade loves _listening to music_ , but she doesn't like _____ .

2 Ben enjoys _____ , but he doesn't like _____ .

3 Jade likes _____ , but she loves _____ .

4 Ben loves _____ , but he doesn't like _____ .

3 (About Me) Answer the questions.

1 Do you like playing table tennis?

_____

2 Do you like playing the guitar?

_____

3 Do you like making lunch?

_____

4 Do you like washing clothes?

_____

4 Think Look and write the verbs on the lists.

do

1 _do homework_
2 _____
3 _____

make

4 _____
5 _____
6 _____

play

7 _____
8 _____
9 _____

5 About Me Look at activity 4. Write sentences.

1 I _____ in the afternoon.
2 I _____ on Saturdays.
3 I like _____ , but _____ .
4 I enjoy _____ , but _____ .

At the market

1 Look and do the word puzzle.

Across →

1 2 3
4 5 6

Down ↓

7 8 9

```
                    7   8
              1  l  e  m  o  n  s
                       
                       
          9            
       2               
                       
       3               
   4                   
                       
   5                   
                       
   6                   
```

2 🗨 Think **Circle the word that is different. Write a sentence about it.**

1 lemons   limes   (onions)   oranges   *Onions are vegetables.*

2 mangoes   snails   limes   grapes   _____

3 carrots   peas   pineapples   _____

4 bananas   pears   sandwiches   _____

3 🗨 About Me **Answer the questions.**

1 What's your favourite fruit?

My favourite _____

2 What colour are they?

_____

3 Are they big or small?

_____

My picture dictionary → Go to page 91 : Find and write the new words.

4 Read and circle the correct pictures.

1 There are lots of pineapples.

2 There are some onions.

3 There aren't any tomatoes.

4 There are lots of mangoes.

5 Look and complete the sentences with *lots of*, *some* or *not any*.

1 There _____*aren't any*_____ onions.

2 There _____ vegetables.

3 There _____ bananas.

4 There _____ tomatoes.

5 There _____ carrots.

6 Look and tick *yes* or *no*.

		Yes, there are.	No, there aren't.
1	Are there any apples?	☐	✔
2	Are there any carrots?	☐	☐
3	Are there any mangoes?	☐	☐
4	Are there any beans?	☐	☐
5	Are there any watermelons?	☐	☐

7 Look at activity 6. Complete the questions and answers.

1 _____Are there any_____ grapes?   _Yes, there are._

2 _____ coconuts?   _____

3 _____ lemons?   _____

4 _____ pineapples?   _____

5 _____ oranges?   _____

Skills: *Writing*

8 **Read the paragraph and write the words.**

> any   aren't   ~~favourite~~   juice   like   some

My ¹___favourite___ smoothie is Tropical Yum. I like orange ²_____ .
It's in my favourite smoothie. Bananas are my favourite fruit. There are
³_____ bananas in my smoothie. There aren't ⁴_____ limes.
I don't ⁵_____ them. They ⁶_____ sweet.

9 (About Me) **Answer the questions.**

1 What's your favourite smoothie? Can you think of a name for it?
My favourite smoothie is _____

2 What juice do you like? Is it in your smoothie?

_____

3 Make a list of the fruit in your smoothie.

_____

4 What fruit don't you like in your smoothie?

_____

10 (About Me) **Write about your favourite smoothie.**

My favourite smoothie _____

_____

_____

_____

_____

_____

11 (About Me) **Ask and answer with a friend.**

> What's your favourite smoothie?   My favourite smoothie is …

12 **Read and write the words.**

are got ~~lots of~~ red one haven't got

There are ___lots of___ handbags.

We _____ any money.

There _____ lots of old clothes in here.

Great! Let's look for a handbag!

Yes! Look!

She's _____ two handbags!

Which handbag do you want?

The _____ .

13 **Look at activity 12. Circle the answers.**

1 They're looking for a _____ .
   a handbag   **b** guitar   **c** hat

2 They haven't got any _____ .
   a shoes   **b** old clothes   **c** money

3 There are lots of _____ .
   a new clothes   **b** big clothes   **c** old clothes

4 Anna's got _____ .
   a an old handbag **b** two handbags   **c** two red handbags

5 Lily wants the _____ .
   a blue handbag **b** red handbag   **c** new handbag

14 **Look and tick the pictures that show the value: reuse old things.**

15 **Draw the shapes around the words with the same sound.**

☐ = sh ◯ = ch

What parts of plants can we eat?

1 Find the words and write under the pictures.

pragse   nabasan   sepa   insono   torcars

grapes

2 Look at activity 1. Read and complete the sentences.

1 They're seeds. They're small. They're green. They're _peas_ .

2 They're roots. They're orange. Rabbits like eating them. They're _____ .

3 They're purple fruit. We can't buy one. We buy lots of them. They're _____ .

4 They're stems. They're long. We don't eat them for breakfast. They're _____ .

5 They're yellow fruit. Monkeys enjoy eating them. They're _____ .

Evaluation

1 **Colour the fruit and vegetables. Then answer the questions.**

1 Are there any apples? _Yes, there are._

2 Are there any pears? _____

3 Are there any carrots? _____

4 Are there any grapes? _____

5 Are there any watermelons? _____

6 Are there any pineapples? _____

2 **Write about your classroom.**

pencils desks flowers ~~books~~ rabbits windows

1 There are lots of ___books___ .   **4** _____

2 There are some _____ .   **5** _____

3 There aren't any _____ .   **6** _____

3 **Complete the sentences about this unit.**

1 I can talk about _____ .

2 I can write about _____ .

3 My favourite part is _____ .

4 **Guess what it is.**

Go to page 93 and circle the answer.

1 Look and write the words. Then colour the picture.

1 Above the sea is a yellow ___sun___ .

2 Next to the towel is a _____ . Colour it pink.

3 On the towel are some red and white _____ .

4 Can you see some _____ ? Colour them blue.

2 Find and circle. Then match and write the words.

chipsswimsuitseatowelsandburger

1

2

3

___chips___

4

5

6

My picture dictionary → Go to page 92: Find and write the new words.

3 Think **Look and write the words.**

hers   his   mine   ours   ~~theirs~~   yours

1   Which umbrella is ___theirs___ ? The red one.

2   Which umbrella is _____ ? The purple one.

3   Which sock is _____ ? The white one.

4   Which sock is _____ ? The yellow one.

5   Which hat is _____ ?

6   The green one's _____ .

4 **Look and answer the questions.**

1   Which shell is his?   *The yellow one's his.*

2   Which shell is hers?   _____

3   Which towel is theirs?   _____

4   Which towel is ours?   _____

5   Which rabbit is mine?   _____

Grammar **75**

5 **Look and circle the answers.**

Whose jacket is (that) / this?
(It's) / They're Ana's.

Whose shoes are these / those?
It's / They're theirs.

Whose bags are these / those?
It's / They're yours.

Whose sunglasses are these / those?
It's / They're mine.

Whose house is this / that?
It's / They're ours.

6 **Look and complete the questions and answers.**

_____Whose_____ hat _____is this_____ ?

It's his.

_____ bike _____ ?

_____ Tim's.

_____ paintings _____ ?

_____ mine.

_____ pencils _____ ?

_____ theirs.

Skills: *Writing*

7 **Read the postcard and answer the questions.**

1 Where is Melvin?   *At the beach.*
2 What does he like doing in the morning?

3 Who does he enjoy playing with?

4 What does he do in the afternoon?

5 What does he eat for lunch?

> Dear Coraline,
>   We are having a lovely holiday. We're at the beach.
>   I like flying my kite in the morning. I enjoy playing with my sister. In the afternoon, I swim in the sea. It is lovely. There are lots of people swimming in the sea. But there aren't any sharks. ☺
>   At lunchtime we go to the café. I eat sausages and chips.
>   See you soon,
>   Melvin

8 (About Me) **Imagine you are on holiday. Answer the questions.**

1 Where are you?   *I'm*
2 Who is on holiday with you?

3 What do you do in the morning?

4 What do you do in the afternoon?

5 What do you eat?

9 (About Me) **Write a postcard to a friend.**

Dear

I am having a

10 (About Me) **Ask and answer with a friend.**

What do you do on holiday?   I swim in the sea.

11 Read and match.

> 1 Hello. Have you got my seven things?
> 2 We hope you enjoy it!
> 3 Good idea. Let's ask my dad.
> 4 Thank you, Mr Lin.

a How shall we get to the cinema?

Let's go by car.

_____

b _____

Wait a minute! Whose car is that?

It's Aunt Pat's.

c 1

Aunt Pat!

d Welcome to our show!

_____

12 Look at activity 11. Circle the answers.

1 Where do they go?
   a to the supermarket   b to the school   **c to the cinema**

2 How do they get there?
   a by bike   b by car   c by bus

3 How many things have they got?
   a three   b five   c seven

4 Whose things are they?
   a Lily's   b Aunt Pat's   c Mr Lin's

5 What are the things for?
   a family and friends   b Anna   c a show

13 Look and write the answers. Then tick the picture that shows the value: appreciate your family and friends.

Thank you!   ~~Dinner is ready!~~   Five minutes, Mum!   You are a great dad!

① Dinner is ready!

②

14 Circle the words that sound like *dolphin*.

 ①

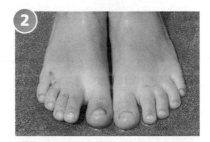 ②

 ③

 ④

 ⑤

 ⑥

 ⑦

 ⑧

 ⑨

Are sea animals symmetrical?

1 **Look and write the words.**

crab   jellyfish   octopus   sea horse   ~~shell~~   starfish

1
shell

2

3

4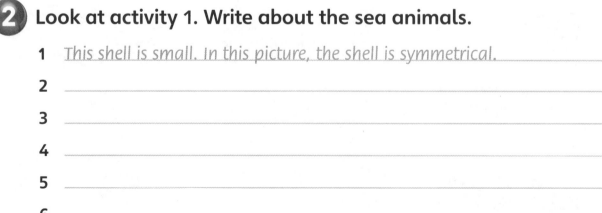

5

6

2 **Look at activity 1. Write about the sea animals.**

1   This shell is small. In this picture, the shell is symmetrical.

2

3

4

5

6

Evaluation

1 **Look and do the word puzzle.**

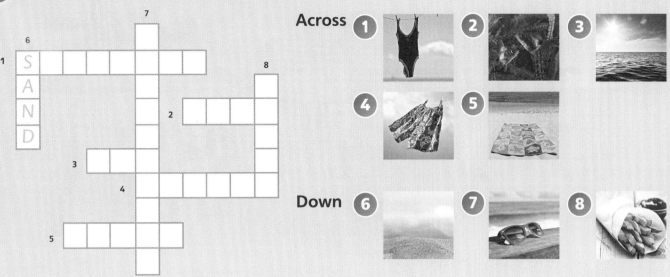

Across 1 2 3 4 5

Down 6 7 8

2 **Look and circle the answers.**

1 Whose bag is this?
It's hers / his.

2 Which hat is his?
It's the white one. /
It's the red one.

3 Whose ball is this?
It's his / hers.

4 Which jacket is hers?
It's the green one. /
It's the blue one.

3 **(About Me)** **Complete the sentences about this unit.**

1 I can talk about _____ .

2 I can write about _____ .

3 My favourite part is _____ .

4 **(Puzzle)** **Guess what it is.**

Go to page 93 and circle the answer.

Review Units 7 and 8

1 Look and answer the questions.

1 Are there any shorts? _____Yes, there are._____

2 Are there any sunglasses? _____

3 Are there any shells? _____

4 Is there a swimsuit? _____

5 Is there a towel? _____

6 Are there any pineapples? _____

7 Are there any lemons? _____

8 Is there a watermelon? _____

9 Are there any onions? _____

10 Are there any coconuts? _____

2 Look and match. Complete the sentences with *some*, *lots of* or *not any*.

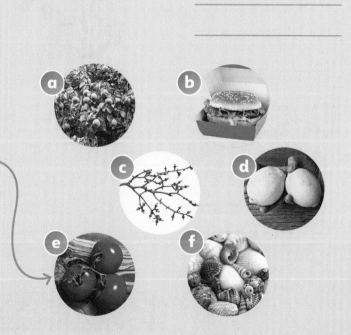

1 _There are some_ tomatoes.

2 _____ pears.

3 _____ lemons.

4 _____ shells.

5 _____ grapes.

6 _____ chips.

3 Look and circle the words.

1 Whose pineapple is (this) / that?

(It's) / They're yours.

2 Whose onions are these / those?

It's / They're yours.

3 Whose limes are these / those?

It's / They're mine.

4 Whose shell is this / that?

It's / They're mine.

4 Think Look and circle the words. Then answer the questions.

1 Which camera is hers / (yours)?

The small one's mine.

2 Which kite is his / yours?

_____

3 Which pencil case is his / ours?

_____

4 Which towel is his / theirs?

_____

5 Which bag is hers / his?

_____

Welcome

Lucas ~~Anna~~ Max Tom Lily

Anna ___ ___ ___ ___

March December ~~January~~ August April October
June November May February July September

J a n u a r y	F _ _ _ _ _ _	M _ _ _ _
A _ _ _ _	M _ _	J _ _ _
J _ _ _	A _ _ _ _ _	S _ _ _ _ _ _
O _ _ _ _ _ _	N _ _ _ _ _ _	D _ _ _ _ _ _

snail   guinea pig   caterpillar   tortoise   ~~butterfly~~
tree   flower   grass   rabbit   leaf

butterfly

2 At school

reception   library   sports field   classroom   gym   Music room
dining hall   ~~Art room~~   playground   Science room

Art room

Saturday   Tuesday   ~~Monday~~   Thursday
Sunday   Wednesday   Friday

M o n d a y

T

W

T

F

S

S

4 My day

go to school   get up   have a shower   have breakfast   get dressed
have lunch   go home   have dinner   ~~clean your teeth~~   go to bed

clean your teeth

5 Home time

do homework   watch TV   ~~do the dishes~~   listen to music   wash the car
play on the computer   drink juice   make a cake   read a book   eat a sandwich

do the dishes

6 Hobbies

play the recorder   play table tennis   do karate   play badminton   make models
play the guitar   make films   play the piano   ~~do gymnastics~~   play volleyball

do gymnastics

_____

_____

_____

_____

_____

_____

_____

_____

_____

onions ~~coconuts~~ watermelons mangoes pineapples
tomatoes limes pears lemons grapes

coconuts

8 At the beach

swimsuit   chips   shells   sun   ~~burger~~   sunglasses   sand   towel   sea   shorts

burger

Puzzle

1 Find the words ↓ →. Then use the coloured letters to answer the question.

P	G	L	I	B	R	A	R	Y	A	R	C	U	B
I	Q	E	R	T	G	Y	J	K	E	L	P	V	E
N	L	A	B	U	T	T	E	R	F	L	Y	U	V
E	B	Z	M	S	W	L	H	B	G	T	D	A	M
A	M	N	F	O	T	D	W	B	I	I	S	O	A
P	G	O	A	O	S	H	O	W	E	R	H	X	T
P	A	A	N	M	G	I	R	C	M	Q	E	Z	H
L	J	G	N	H	K	L	U	Y	O	O	L	P	S
E	M	U	A	N	T	U	E	R	N	S	L	L	Y
X	V	I	E	B	G	H	Y	O	P	W	F	R	Y
D	O	T	H	E	D	I	S	H	E	S	O	K	R
J	K	A	S	K	V	B	Y	U	K	E	T	R	E
M	I	R	W	T	E	C	J	F	H	A	N	N	A

Q: What are two things people can't eat before breakfast?

A: _ _ _ _ _ _   and   _ _ _ _ _ _ _ _ !

Story fun

1 Match the objects to the words. Then match the words to the story units they come from.

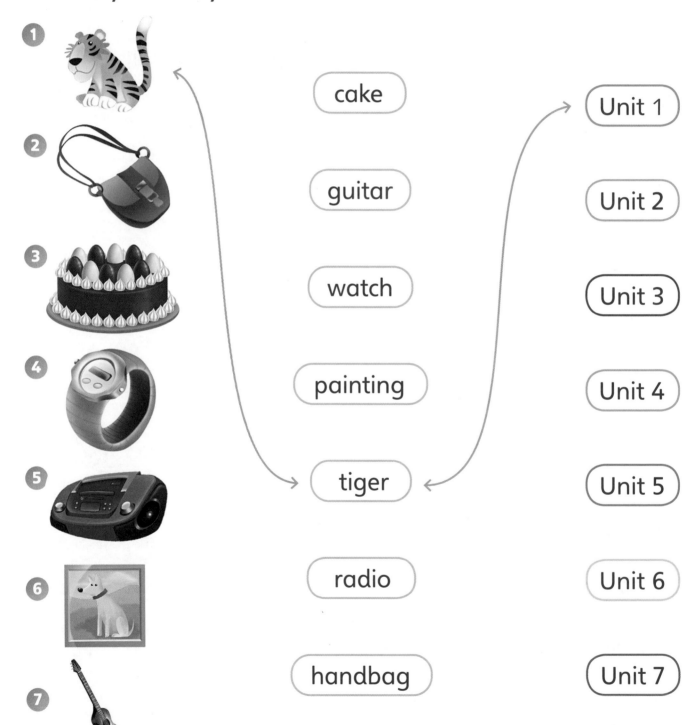

cake

guitar

watch

painting

tiger

radio

handbag

Unit 1

Unit 2

Unit 3

Unit 4

Unit 5

Unit 6

Unit 7

Write the numbers in the box of the objects in Aunt Pat's show.